FROM
GRIEF TO
GREATNESS

Tom Sweetman

Written by Tom Sweetman
Edited by James Moore
Cover Design by Ro Ducay
http://www.hazegraypixels.com

I would like to thank everyone who has inpsired me in life. This book is in honour of my mum with all my heart, my family, my friends and is written to assist anyone who is experiencing grief right now. My purpose with the book was to help at least 1 other person may you find some inspiration from my journey and those I have met.

Come visit my online home
http://www.tomletgo.com

Download your free copy of my quote book Words through grief.
htttp://www.tomletgo.com/wordsthroughgrief

Join Our Free - Monthly Grief Hangouts
http://www.tomletgo.com/griefhangout

Contents

Introduction

I want to thank you for downloading From Grief To Greatness. This book contains real life stories from people just like you and me who experienced grief and shared the lessons they have learned from this experience.

Grief is really the unspoken for many people. After my experience of the death of my mum I wanted to let my grief be spoken.

"It is painful, it is raw and it has the ability to bring a grown man to his knees. It is a lonely journey and a shadow that will encompass all. My God, grief is a monster! You feel no remorse and you leave me in fear, a brutal teacher I cannot escape. The seconds feel like minutes, the minutes feel like hours, and the hours feel like days. Oh, when will this grief go away?" The grief I am in when I say these things to myself is intense. When others approach I think, "What will you say? Go away, really, what good can come from anything you have to say?" This is a real case of damned if you do and damned if you don't.

I feel so much anger but have nowhere to go. I feel so sad that it feels as if I cannot continue.

Sleepless nights would follow. I would feel unsettled, forgetful and have no appetite. Facing all of this would lead to distress. Tears were shed and with each tear I'd break down a little more. Dreams were now memories and these memories would now fade.

This is an excerpt from my diary, Spring 2012. I want to share my thoughts and feelings so you know you're not alone.

"Definition of Grief – Hardship, suffering, pain. From the Latin – Graver make heavy, weighty. PHRASES: *Loss causes hardship, pain, mental suffering, burden, misfortune and grief.*"

Me and Mum 2011

Chapter 1: Grief From Loss And Death

Loss and Death naturally create grief. Grief is the experience and cycle we go through as a result.

In addition to the emotional pain, grief has the ability to cause any or all of the following feelings and symptoms:

- Physically drained
- Depressed
- Anger
- Lack of appetite
- Loneliness
- Distress
- Forgetfulness
- Confusion

Do you feel like a rollercoaster going up and down torn by regret maybe guilt mixed with grief? Have you asked yourself questions like the ones below?

- Why did this happen?
- What about God?
- He/She was such a good person, why did they have to die?
- He/She was so young, why them?
- How is this fair?

Let me speak with you directly. I believe these questions we ask ourselves are grief. I know from the death of my mum how painful, and upsetting this can be. I want you to know this is normal. Those thoughts of uncertainty are painful and overwhelming.

I'd like to share this little story with you…

I remember the times when this would become too much, I would walk to the beach and shout at the top of my voice, "Why, why is this happening?" The very last thing I remember shouting was, "THIS IS JUST SHIT!!!" Of course, I thought no one was around then I noticed a guy walking his dog. I walked up the beach past him hoping that he wouldn't say a word when he simply said, "Feel's better, doesn't it?" He smiled and continued on his way. I stopped for a moment and thought for that split second when I expressed myself I felt a release; a moment of ease.

Grief is natural. You are human, your pain is raw and it just plain hurts.

Chapter 2: Grief In The World

One thing about grief is it can come from any loss we experience in our life. The most painful time it hit me was from the death of my mum. When it is someone so close or we have known for a long time we have an attachment and connection with them. One thing I found was people don't know how you are feeling. Straight after, my body experienced the shock and numbness that comes from such an event. Then, over time this turns to yearning for my mum or me thinking she would appear like she had for many years. I couldn't relax or sit still so my sleep was affected. Dreams turned into nightmares which awoke me in the middle of the night in shock.

We will all face loss and grief in our lives. In a world where everything is speeding up with technology, work and the modern world we are reaching a tipping point where more and more people who are grieving are feeling more and more isolated. There are so many distractions to take you away from pain that today it is easier to fill our voids with temporary fixes such as food, alcohol, obsessions or drugs which hide the pain you are truly experiencing. Later, this can lead to severe problems in a person's mental health. Being stuck in denial of death can lead to depression as the person keeps deluding themselves in an attempt to not upset themselves or any other loved ones.

The world is changing at such a fast pace and with the amount of loss and death happening I want to use the experience of my pain plus these stories I have collected from others to show you it is possible to face and transform your grief. When you read the statistics below you will realise how many of us are facing loss, separation and death. We are not the only ones suffering, it is just we are suffering alone.

There were 484,367 deaths registered in England and Wales in 2011. 30% of the deaths were from cancer. (*Office of National Statistics.*)

In the United States, 8 million people suffered through the death of someone in their immediate family last year. There were 800,000 new widows and widowers; additionally, 400,000 people under the age of 25 suffered from the death of a loved one. (*National Mental Health Association.*)

The number of divorces in England and Wales in 2011 was 117,558, a decrease of 1.7% since 2010, where there were 119,589 divorces.

Chapter 3: Grief Is An Opportunity

Maybe that sounds challenging at this moment in time. If someone had said that to me when my Mum passed away I would have said it wasn't possible. But wait, let me ask you this…

Would you like to be able to:

— *Use your pain in a positive way?*
— *Speak about the one you loss with gratitude and love?*
— *Use your pain to assist others?*
— *Transform the pain you are in from not affecting your everyday life?*
— *Understand more clearly and even find the positives of your loss?*
— *Discover who you are and what you are here to do?*
— *Live the rest of your life knowing why your loved one had to go and being able to honour them, as well?*
— *Find the love and connection in your life again?*
— *Turn your grief into greatness?*

There is a bridge the gap from grief to greatness and from pain to love. Leaving you in a place of:

— *Balance and clarity*
— *Openness*
— *A new awareness of loss and death*
— *Gratitude*
— *Love*
— *Inspiration*
— *Appreciation of your loved one and the ability to move forward with less pain*

I believe you can be set free to honour the person you truly are and be restored to love and life. Return to that place of authenticity without grief, guilt fear and shame.

This is the new opportunity...

Chapter 4: My Story

I feel the best way to begin healing is openness and I want to share with you what led me to writing this book you are now reading.

During April 2011, I was attending a workshop where a speaker discussed how we can empower different aspects of our lives. One audience member was speaking about the grief that was still haunting them after the death of their mother from cancer a few years ago.

Because my Mum was diagnosed with breast cancer in 2008, I was hooked and wanted to hear more. Their story really moved me as I knew this could have been my Mum who had passed away from cancer.

What happened next was unfathomable. After just having attended a lecture about death and grief, 5 minutes later my phone rang, and it was my Dad.

He called to inform me that my Mum's cancer had returned, and it was aggressive and terminal. It was now in the bone, liver as well as the breast.

It was in that moment that I knew my life was never going to be the same again. Fear, guilt, worry, and shock plagued me. My thoughts were racing. I wondered, "How long does she have? How will my sisters cope? How will my Gran be?"

It was almost like the world that was once full of bliss and opportunities was now relegated to a dark, empty box that I was crouched in. I shortly decided to move back from London where I had been living and relocate to Devon so I could be closer to my Mum and Dad. I felt like my Mum had always been my rock and now it was my turn to do that for her.

As time passed, my Mum's health got worse and worse. We were fortunate to spend a beautiful but emotional last Christmas together as family. Then, soon into the New Year, my Mum was transferred into St. Luke's Hospice.

The following 3 months were a stressful time of self-reflection and fear with my Mum facing life and death every day. Many people that my Mum encountered there passed away quickly. I spent the time there recording my thoughts, trying to remember my journey so that it could help me heal.

During the last week of my Mum's life, she was becoming very weak, and we all knew her time coming to an end. However, one thing that gave me strength was when she told me, "Tom I did everything I wanted. I travelled the world. I had 3 wonderful kids and a loving husband and family, I have no regrets, and I want you to be the best you can be. Look after everyone, and live with no regrets too."

Mum passed a week after. She had been in a lot of pain for many months, but she was resting well when she passed. The following months were very hard but also very enlightening. At Mum's funeral the church was so busy there was not room for everyone. Once the funeral was over, adjusting to normal life was difficult.

I spent a lot of time in self-discovery, and I noticed that I felt a transformation within me. I soon realised my pain had become my gift. I would start to share with others who were facing loss and grief my realisations and noticed more people were attracted to what I was saying by finding the truth within what I had learned. It was through this my gift was awakened to transform the experience of grief, loss and death to assisting others unlock their greatness.

Between you and I my intention for this book is to assist you on your journey through grief and to show you a different way of seeing loss. Pain can be our biggest teacher and I will reveal to you how you can not only grow and learn from it but also use it to unlock a connection and purpose in life that you have inside waiting to serve the world.

Throughout this book and the stories you hear you will learn through other's experiences and real life stories the following:

- L.O.V.E
- Compassion
- Pain Is Temporary
- Discovering Your Gift
- The Truth About Honesty
- Everything In Life Is A Present
- Facing Your Shadow
- The Power Of Non-Verbal Communication
- Getting Rid Of Anger And Guilt
- The Courage Of Vulnerability
- The Acceptance Of What Is
- Live A Life Of Meaning

- Understand The Ego
- Letting Go – How To Give Up
- Have A Connection To The Loved One You Lost And Loved Ones In Your Life
- How to Use Your Pain To Serve Others
- Discover Your Values And Purpose

Chapter 5: Current State

Grief is a sensitive issue and an issue we all face. These are my experiences and the truth of my journey and studies in this area. My words are simply signposts for you to guide you back into your own truth.

I define grief as the emotional suffering caused from the loss of someone or something significant in your life. The more intense the suffering the more emotionally attached we usually were to that person.

What I noticed is grief is a uniquely individual experience. We all have different experiences, however, there are some common themes that I believe do not change.

If you ignore grief and the pain it causes it will not just go away and disappear. In fact, what can happen is it resurfaces in another aspect or area of your life months or even years down the line. Crying is not the only form of expressing grief. I had many days I would just be hurting so badly inside that I couldn't even express it.

With millions of us facing grief every year it was so scary to find out how lonely the journey is and how disconnected people are on this subject. Here is a little test. Think of one famous singer? Okay how long did that take?

Now think of a famous grief specialist? I guess you didn't come up with one that quickly right?

Why? Because we hide things in society we find difficult to face. Yet behind closed doors we are suffering and we all struggle with it at some point. Grief isn't on our main TV networks, magazines or radios.

You may have even heard these words before, "You have to move on" or "You have to move forward." How hurtful these words can be but people simply know no better. When we sweep death and grief under the carpet that's what happens.

Western Society has become more about *me* and less about *us*.

In this book I want to reveal the power of serving and giving that is within us all.

Society is much more focused on keeping up appearances, pretending everything is fine when inside it's not. Think about how many times someone says, "Hello, how are you?" Your automatic response is, "I'm fine, and you?" This answer becomes a barrier to what is really happening. It becomes a block to the real feelings going on inside but for some reason we feel it best to keep it to ourselves. When Mum died I'd say those words and just keep going. I felt like I didn't want to burden anyone with my problem and other times I didn't think anyone would understand what I was going through.

When you experience a loss the grief is painful and raw.

Tip From Tom:

HUG.

A simple hug has the power to transcend words and communicate love. I don't care if you're a man or a woman or whether you worry if others think it is cool or not. We all need a hug. If you don't know what to say to someone who is in grief then give them a hug. You always have the ability to share that. It is free and the biggest gift you can give someone, aside from your time and love.

The stages of grief seem to follow a pattern and without confining it to a small box. I really feel the psychiatrist Elisabeth Kübler-Ross share a great analysis of the stages we go through.

Kübler-Ross' 5 Stages of Grief:

- **Denial:** "This can't be happening to me."
- **Anger:** "Why is this happening?
- **Bargaining:** "Make this not happen, and in return I will ____."
- **Depression:** "I'm so sad…
- **Acceptance:** "I'm at peace with what happened."

The process is natural and we go through it in our own ways but sometimes without assistance we can really get stuck with out grief and caught up in a vicious cycle that will burden us and cause us months if not years of suffering.

Chapter 6: Grief Is Universal

As I mentioned briefly in the Introduction the world is changing. We are now connected to information and opportunities globally through the Internet and the power of technology. Grief is lonely and I found once my Mum had passed away and the funeral was over, I was alone with my thoughts and pain. It wasn't until I had worked through and transformed my grief that I came across some inspiring and resourceful ways technology was being used.

You can now speak with others experiencing grief living eight thousand miles away. This power to connect opens you up to knowing there are many people just like you suffering.

One amazing example of bringing people together who are in various stages of grief is a Facebook group called *Grief The Unspoken* run by Angie Cartwright. Angie wanted to use her grief to connect with others online and started sharing her experience through a Facebook page. Over the last few years the group has increased to several thousand members who act as a support group for each other with one thing in common. They are experiencing grief.

When I discovered the group I found it so amazing and was relieved that people could begin sharing their grief with others who would listen and have a connection to what was happening. It has allowed many people to open up from the safety of their own home. I believe this has become an important place for people to connect, especially at the most raw time in their stages of grief. It becomes a form of compassion and counselling from a peer group, at no cost to anyone and yet maintains safety behind the comfort of a computer screen. *www.facebook.com/ grieftheunspoken*

Another example of how times are changing is right now in your very hands. This book that I am writing for you from my experience is only possible because I'm able to use technology to access much of the needed information via the Web. Years ago it was only a few authors getting published and now I have the ability with lower costs to use my pain and experience to share with you the powerful methods to transform the grief you are in to something great. At the end of the book I have provided some great online resources for you to have a look at to aid you in your journey from grief to greatness that I, myself have found useful. Please also visit *www.tomletgo.com* and fill in your name and email to receive your free From Grief to Greatness picture book and interviews on the topic of grief.

Chapter 7: Grief Is Natural

Grief is a natural process. It is becoming more clearly recognised as people share their personal journeys and stories. What I have come to realise is that there is actually opportunity working through grief. You may be thinking at this stage…opportunity?

Yes, grief truly presents an opportunity. I want to share with you one person who experienced more grief than you or I will most likely ever face.

The gentleman in question is Dr. Victor Frankl.

Psychiatrist Viktor Frankl's memoir has riveted generations of readers with its descriptions of life in the Nazi death camps and its lessons for spiritual survival.

Between 1942 and 1945, Frankl laboured in four different camps, including Auschwitz, while his parents, brother, and pregnant wife perished. Based on his own experience and the experiences of those he treated in his practice, Frankl argues that we cannot avoid suffering but we can choose how to cope with it, find meaning in it, and move forward with renewed purpose. Frankl's theory—known as logotherapy, from the Greek word logos—means that which holds our primary drive in life is not pleasure, as Freud maintained, but the discovery and pursuit of what we personally find meaningful.

So for three years, this man went through pain, torture and grief losing his parents, brother, and pregnant wife, but he made a choice he was either going to give up or make it through. He used his pain to survive and went on to inspire a generation. He sold 10 million copies of his book Man's Search for Meaning.

This book certainly changed my life and I kept a copy of it during my Mum's last few weeks and finished it after her passing. It made me realise we are all facing grief. It is painful but also there is something more and deeper to our lives. Victor showed me that it is possible to heal and to change my experience. He showed me that someone who had lost people could continue to live a powerful and enriched life. And that gives me hope.

Ever since my journey of grief led me to writing this book, I have noticed and become so aware that grief is becoming more and more talked about. I see more and more people talking about the subject of death, loss and grief from local papers, radio shows and magazines. Maybe, just maybe we are bringing the issue that will affect us all to mainstream attention. I feel this positive step will help many, many people. My gift to you is to share as much of my journey as openly and honestly with you in the hope that it will leave a positive impact upon your journey through grief.

One big step for me in facing the subject was to sit down and write this book. It has enabled me to research and face my own darkness and confront certain aspects of my life that I never realised grief was affecting. When my Mum left it felt like a part of my life vanished. There was a complete emptiness. What really struck me was hundreds of thousands of people leave us every year but we only grieve for the ones who had an impact on our lives.

The problem with loss is it can leave us feeling incomplete and trying to fill our incompleteness with things, people or jobs. We all grieve anything that leaves a hole in our lives.

Disabled by grief, overwhelmed by loss to the extent that normal coping processes are disabled or shut down, grief counselling facilitates expression of emotion and thought about the loss, including sadness, anxiety, anger, loneliness, guilt, relief, isolation, confusion, or numbness.

Chapter 8: The Journey Of Grief

When faced with grief and going through the process there are so many different ways that we grieve and get ourselves back into healing and living again. I believe after my experience, there is no right or wrong way unless you are hurting yourself or others.

Grief takes us to many dark corners we don't want to face or deal with. First we enter the hard wall of denial, blocking out the fact that the person has left and not accepting that it is actually happening. From my experience, it felt like shock, a disbelief of the current situation almost as if you're watching it happen to someone else. The problem of denial is it can block you from healing, make you delusional and trapped in the past. Almost like the child who had broken a very special family dish, then hid the fact they did it by convincing themselves it wasn't them (compulsive lying).

For me denial crept in during the mornings when I awoke, just after my Mum passed away. After so many years of having someone around, you never even consider they may not be there so you replay a normal routine, but this time when you walk into the house and call out your Mum's name, there is no answer. You quickly cover it up and continue to avoid the reality that at some point must be accepted and block out the truth.

The following emotion that grief caused me was anger. The "why is this happening" moments; the ones when your body is tense, you feel lost, desperate, the world owes you and it's not fair.

I would now like to invite you to meet some people just like you and me who have faced grief. Through these stories my hope is you will be able to relate to and learn from them sharing openly their experience of grief. For me, grief is not really spoken about in society. People are comfortable talking about pleasure but never pain. So as I like to say, let the grief be spoken.

Chapter 9: Grief Lesson Stories - Nicola Simpson – Abigail's Rainbow

Grief Lesson Story

Hi, I'm Nicola Simpson author of Abigail's Rainbow. I don't see myself as a writer, yet I'm a bestselling author. All I wanted was to share my story to help others. My daughter Abigail tragically died in a car accident in 2007 on her way to a party. I live every parents' worst nightmare along with my husband and our younger daughter Hannah. Our lives were torn apart and destroyed. A young man's simple mistake, speeding and inexperienced he lost control of his car, taking my daughter's life.

I now spend my time travelling the world, sharing my story, holding workshops and am often invited to speak at events. I feel that this is my life purpose. Something amazing has come from the worst possible thing ever... my daughter died.

What your site/project purpose is:

Abigail's Rainbow website and Facebook pages are aimed to help, encourage and inspire others facing grief to know that it's ok to feel the way we do while we're grieving. The pain and emotions are normal but also, the smiles too. Happiness seems impossible in times of despair but one day when you're ready your own beautiful smile can return.

My drive behind writing and sharing was that there is someone else out there suffering, feeling alone and in despair just like I was. I wanted to reach out and help. I often say that my book is the hand that reaches into that dark depressing tunnel. It doesn't say I'll pull you out or I can make things better. It's the hand that reaches in to let you know you're not alone.

The first chapter of Abigail's Rainbow is available to read at *http://www.abigailsrainbow.com/*. It's a very raw account of my journey through grief.

Your Story of Grief

6th October 2007, the worst day of my life. 11:20pm a policeman knocked at my door. Abigail was late home, she'd left to go out with her friends to a party.

Her friend Scott had just passed his driving test three days earlier. He hadn't been drinking and offered to give Abigail and her friends a lift to the party. Young, foolish and inexperienced he allowed one friend to get in the boot of his car so that the three girls would fit in the back. Scott drove himself and his five passengers to Castletown in Caithness, Scotland. He and his friend overtook each other several times along the main rural road towards the village. Speeding as he approached the reduce speed signs he continued into the village and lost control of his car. Scott's vehicle clipped the kerb and hit a pillar at the end of the wall. Abigail sitting in the rear of the car took full impact and died there at the scene. My fifteen-year-old daughter gone from this world forever.

In that moment as I heard the policeman tell my husband Paul and I that our daughter had died my own soul left me. I was left with an emptiness and numbness inside. I no longer existed. Time stood still. I was breathing but not living.

I have been to the deepest darkest place while grieving, I wanted to end my life a thousand times over. The suicidal thoughts were scary and at times I felt I mentally barricaded myself in my home so that I didn't do it. I have a life to live and a story to share. I need to stay in this world so that I can help others to know that it's ok to feel this way when we're grieving.

So many of us feel alone, that no-one understands. But, in fact, there are thousands of us out there grieving, all in our own way, all in pain and some suffering silently.

I moved to Cyprus with my family and began to write, sharing my deepest darkest moments, the pain, and the torment. But while writing the most amazing thing happened, I found forgiveness. It's such an incredible feeling. The weight has lifted and I am now able to live a fulfilling life once more. I will always miss my daughter but I no longer live with that deep heart wrenching pain of grief. I feel I have faced every pain and emotion known to human kind.

I now live with a spring in my step and a smile on my face and know that my life is worth living. When I look back six years I would never have thought this was possible, but now I know it is. I use what I have learnt to now help and inspire others so that they too can move forward in their bereavement towards a more fulfilling life again. We will never forget our loved ones, we will always miss them but we have a life of our own to lead too.

What is the main lesson grief taught you about living?

To help me face my grief I searched for help. I've been through counselling, talking and sharing my inner most pain with a stranger helped me to release.

I went to see a spiritualist for crystal healing and later learnt self-healing. I discovered yoga and meditation and found this helped me tremendously; a place of stillness and peace when my mind was a mess, my thoughts and pain never leaving me.

My journey through grief has taken me on a spiritual realisation about myself. I've found the person that I really am deep inside. I've found my peace with grief, the physical pain no longer exists, my thoughts are clear and now I am left with my memories, the sad and the happy ones too.

I believe I have found my life purpose through my grieving process. I'm here to help others.

How did you come to find acceptance of the loss?

I was distraught for such a long time, in search of help to deal with the pain that lived within in me emotionally and physically.

I found talking about Abigail really helped me to release. I was very lucky that I lived in a small community where everyone wanted to help. Friends and even strangers would listen to me talk about my daughter and the pain I felt inside. Often sobbing, unable to cope. Deep within me all I wanted to do was die but it was as if the world just wasn't going to let me go.

When I left my job and moved to Cyprus with Paul and Hannah I began to write. I shared with my laptop my inner most thoughts, the real deep pain that was knotted inside me. Slowly I began to release and the nightmares that I lived with each night began to change. As I wrote one part of my pain so that nightmare would stop and a new one would arrive. The more I wrote the more I released. I often found myself at my laptop at 4am, tears rolling down my face unable to see the screen. But I would tap away exactly how I felt in that moment.

Hannah and I returned to Caithness, Scotland in Summer 2011 to see friends and family. But while I was there this thought that had been lingering with me the past four years kept coming to the forefront of my mind. I wanted to see Scott, the driver of the car, the young man who killed my daughter.

I had questions that needed answers. I wanted to know the journey that ended my daughter's life and I wanted to hear it from Scott. But I didn't know if I was ready.

I drove to Castletown where he lived and knocked on his front door. Hours later I left feeling incredible, in fact I felt I'd made history. In those hours I had seen and heard his remorse, the pain he felt. I felt compassion for him. He'd made a stupid mistake, one that devastated two families, one that my daughter paid the highest price for; her life. He didn't mean to kill my baby.

As I left I hugged him as a mother would her son. This was the beginning of my road to forgiveness.

What advice would you give to someone who has experienced loss recently?

Breathe. Quite simply breathe.

There is nothing more in life you need to do right now. You are your focus and those immediately around you, your husband, wife and children. You know who I mean.

Take the time you need to feel the pain. Locking it away inside means that one day in the future it will surface, it's best to release it - let it out.

Scream and shout when you're angry with the world. Not at anyone in particular, just to the universe. I used to go for a drive in my car to the middle of nowhere or a deserted beach to do this. I've screamed in my bedroom and hoped my neighbours wouldn't hear, but in the end I didn't care. I needed to let out my pain.

Cry when you need to, when you feel these emotions bubbling away, let them surface. Give yourself permission to feel it. The more you allow yourself to feel the more you can release.

And if like me you have felt suicidal, ask yourself the question "Do I want to die today or for the rest of my life?"

For me it was always just in that moment, I accepted I wanted to die but I knew I wouldn't feel this way tomorrow.

Get help! You really don't have to suffer your pain alone, there are professionals out there that deal with grief, suicide, healing and the medical profession. There are so many of us in this world suffering and we can help each other.

You're not alone.

Did anyone say anything to you or do anything for you during your time of grief that really helped you?

The biggest help for me was the kindness of others listening. Being allowed to speak freely about my thoughts and feelings, sharing my pain allowed me to let go a little each time. I can honestly say that some days I must have repeated myself over twenty times but fortunately I had met that many people in one day whom I could talk to.

I held back a lot of my inner most pain, the real darkness within me, but by talking I was able to release the layers of pain until I needed help to reach the depths of darkness.

Don't bottle it all up inside, talk and share with someone you can trust.

And if you don't have someone to talk to, write it down as if you were talking to a best friend or trusted relative.

What is your philosophy of grief?

Grief is a natural pain of loss. At some point we're all going to die, those we love and care for and even us. No one is immortal.

There are different forms of grief and pain. Someone once told me "There is no hierarchy for suffering." This is very true.

None of us know what the pain feels like for others, we only know our own. The loss is relative to us, how we felt about the person who has passed away and left this world. The relationship you had with that person is so different to others.

For some during times of prolonged illness it's a welcome relief that they no longer suffer and for others it's complete devastation.

Grief is our own personal pain and suffering that we need to deal with in our own way, with compassion for ourselves. We need to give ourselves permission to grieve in a way that enables us to continue in life.

How has the pain transformed your life in a positive way with how you are now?

Without a doubt I see death differently.

The realisation that we are all going to die one day and we have no idea when or how that is going to happen has made me really realise that we only get one chance in life.

When I'm struggling to make a decision about different opportunities I now sit back and think "What if I were to die today, 3 months or 12 months from now, would I regret having done or not done whatever it is that's bothering me."

Always say goodbye to someone you love and care about and never leave on bad terms, it might just be the last time you see them.

Don't live life with regrets!

Any other lessons you have learnt from grief to share and assist others?

My Do's and Don'ts!!

Let's start with the DONT's:

- If possible don't make any major decisions within the first year of bereavement i.e. move home, buy a new car etc. unless of course you have to.
- Expect your family or friends to grieve the same as you.
- Expect anyone to fully understand what you're going through, your pain, thoughts, feelings and emotions.
- Don't suffer alone.

My Do's:

- Seek help and support from friends, relatives or professional help such as counselling.
- Listen to your body - you know when you're not functioning 100%, allow for this.
- Give yourself permission to grieve, go with the flow of your feelings and emotions and release them.
- Find your own coping mechanisms, you know what you believe in, how you think and feel, work with it. I love booking a one to one boxing session at the gym to release my anger and frustration!!
- Breathe, smile and learn to love your life again.

Website:

http://www.abigailsrainbow.com/

Twitter:

https://twitter.com/NicolaSimpson10

Facebook:

www.facebook.com/AbigailsRainbow

Chapter 10: Grief Lesson Stories - Michelle Cruz Rosado - Inspirational Speaker, Author and Mentor

Grief Lesson Story

I am co-author of the inspirational book, *Pursuing Your Destiny: How to Overcome Adversity and Achieve Your Dreams*, I'm an inspirational speaker, author and mentor.

What your site/project purpose is:

After a period of awakening from overcoming life-changing adversities in my childhood and early adult life I have devoted my life to teaching and mentoring around the world through words of love, hope and perseverance.

Your Story of Grief:

My life was drastically changed on the morning of September 11, 2001. I was working as a presentation specialist for Fiduciary Trust, an investment banking firm located in the upper floors of Tower 2. At 8:43am I was at my desk when I felt the first plane crash into Tower 1.

By taking one of the last elevators before the second plane crashed into Tower 2, I was able to escape the building before its collapse, but lost 85 friends and co-workers that day. Thus began my spiritual journey.

What is the main lesson grief taught you about living?

There were many lessons learned from that experience, the main one being that it is so very important to live in the present moment.

How did you come to find acceptance of the loss?

Only when I began writing and speaking publicly about the experience did I feel there was a full acceptance of my friends' tragic deaths. When I realized that each one of us has a unique purpose, there was no reason to feel guilty about my survival.

What advice would you give to someone who has experienced loss recently?

After the devastating loss of my Mom to cancer last year, I realized that I was not alone, and no one should ever feel that they cannot be comforted by the compassion of another.

Did anyone say anything to you or do anything for you during your time of grief that really helped you?

In the weeks following September 11, I wrote an article entitled, "Will I Recover?" which described my personal experience that day. I emailed it to my friends and former co-workers, and in a month's time the article went viral. I started receiving emails from people around the world who came across my article. One email in particular came from a 15 year-old girl from Australia. I will never forget her words of strength and encouragement, for they motivated me to continue writing and eventually become a professional speaker.

What is your philosophy of grief?

It is within our own time that we grieve, for each one of us has our own way of healing.

How has the pain transformed your life in a positive way with how you are now?

The pain that emerged from the 9/11 tragedy gave me the ability to focus not on myself, but the devotion to healing humanity as a whole.

Any other lessons you have learnt from grief you'd like to share?

To grieve is to know that although we are human, we can connect with our inner Being by releasing the past and embracing the present moment.

Website:

http://MichelleRosado.com

Chapter 11: Grief Lesson Stories - Robin Chodak – Recover Now From Loss

Grief Lesson Story

What your site purpose is:

To sum it up it is a place of hope. Suicide loss is like no other loss. It leaves everyone who has experienced it in a wake of disbelief and questioning. They ask how this could happen and why didn't we know? No one can understand what this type of grief feels like unless they have gone through it themselves. This I do not wish on anyone. Those of us who have had the experience need a place to talk to others and express our thoughts. We know we can do it with those who have gone through it and understand. We do not feel threatened or vulnerable expressing ourselves in a safe place. We can have hope because there are others who have survived and it inspires us to keep moving forward. Since I am a survivor and know it is possible to recover I want to offer encouragement by posting relevant information on my Facebook page.

Your Story of Grief

The grief of losing your loved one is an unbearable experience. I lost my soul mate, my husband Steve, he was my prince, my love, and my everything and in one moment he was gone. I came home from work and found him dead in our basement from multiple gun shots to his head. That in itself put me into a state of shock causing me to suffer PTSD (post-traumatic stress disorder). My life changed forever in that instant. After the shock wore off, I went through the many stages of grief. Anger being one I experienced. The trauma immobilized me and I knew I needed help and found a suicide support group, but was angry that I needed to be in such a place. I was angry at God, angry at my husband and angry at the world. The group helped me to understand my anger and eventually let go of it. The realization that my husband was never coming back caused me to fall into a depression. I wondered how I could manage without him. I didn't know where to begin. I felt inept in all things. I didn't think that I had anything to live for without the man I entangled my life. I had waited for him for 35 years and only had him in my life for 10. It was too short and I began to have serious thoughts about ending my life so I could join him.

Even in the throes of grief my mind still found its way to logical thinking to convince me that suicide was not the answer, unlike my husband who didn't have the ability to think rationally. My thoughts frightened me and I sought out psychotherapy which started me down my road to recovery. I needed to accept that my life would never be the same and that I would need to find ways to survive on my own. I needed to begin to create a new identity for myself. When one's life is wrapped so intimately with another the grief of separation is very difficult and you don't think you will survive. But I am a testimony along with many others that it is possible. It begins with hope and it continues with making healthy choices for your life.

What is the main lesson grief taught you about living?

I always believed that life was a precious gift but after Steve died grief tricked me into thinking it wasn't, thankfully only for a short period of time. Once I arrived at the place of accepting Steve's death I began to treasure living more than I ever had. I have learned that each moment is to be savoured even in the small mundane tasks, such as washing dishes or doing the laundry. I do things now in a mindful way believing there is purpose in everything. I move more slowly and think more deeply about each action I take in life. I realize that each of us have a unique purpose no matter how large or how small. Mine is to encourage others. I can do this with my Facebook page and I can do it at the grocery store by holding a door open or helping an elder person grab an item that is too high for them to reach.

Doing simple acts of kindness give me purpose and can lead others to do the same.

How did you come to find acceptance of the loss?

Acceptance comes through working through your grief. It is not something that can be denied of faked. Many people don't want to do the work because it is very hard to face your feelings and just "be" with them. It is an uncomfortable process, but one that is necessary for healing and moving forward. I learned that grief plays many tricks on a suffering soul. It makes us believe many things that are not true. I realized it was doing that to me and I needed to take grief by the hand and walk with it so I could get through it. Realizing that we have no control over another person's action is key to the acceptance process. We cannot think if we love someone enough it will protect them and they will never do any harm to themselves or us. That is false thinking. Acceptance is realizing that each person chooses to live their lives based on their own terms and who they desire to be, just as we live ours. Acceptance is relinquishing all control over another human being which frees us from any guilt that we may have carried because of the suicide. Psychotherapy and support groups were instrumental in helping me learn acceptance.

What advice would you give to someone who has experienced loss recently?

Don't give up hope. I would let them know that all the emotions they are experiencing are normal and they should not be hard on themselves. Most definitely they need to understand that they are not to blame. Guilt has a way of keeping its victims stuck in their grief. Most survivors feel that they could have somehow prevented the suicide from happening. I thought the same. If I had stayed home from work that day then it would not have happened. I realized later that I could not stay home every day. If he didn't do it that day, he could have found another one to complete it. Survivors must let go of their guilt in order to move forward. I also recommend they seek a support system, either Facebook pages like mine and/or psychotherapy and support groups offered by AFSP (American Foundation for Suicide Prevent) or LOSS (Loving Outreach to Suicide Survivors) offered by Catholic Charities.

What is your philosophy of grief?

I don't believe our culture allows people to process grief in the ways that they should. Often there are times people think you should just "get over it" and "move on." This is a form of denial and only causes problems later on if the anger, guilt, depression, etc., are not dealt with appropriately. If we do not have a chance to recover and heal ourselves how can we be a benefit in society to others? I think there should be an awakening and a shift in our thinking about it. We must not stuff down our grief, we must face it and work it. It is the only way to overcome it.

How has the pain transformed your life in a positive way with how you are now?

I am a changed person because of my husband's suicide. My recovery strengthened me in my faith and I continue on my spiritual journey. I don't believe in the permanence of anything anymore. Everything is a vapour and can dissipate in any moment. Therefore I cherish each and every moment. I believe that all we receive are gifts from God and we should be grateful for the time we have them. I have learned to live with no expectations, because that only leads to disappointments. I have also learned to be less judgmental than I was in my past. Often there are times people say and do harmful things because they are in a very bad state of mind or situation and they need help. I no longer take offense like I used to do. I have learned much and I expect to learn so much more. Each day is a new day to live and love and be thankful. I wake up every day and say, "thank you God."

Any other lessons you have learnt from grief to share and assist others?

It is important to stay positive. When negative thinking bombards your mind it is important to recognize it and remove it quickly and replace it with positive thoughts. I began to say positive words out loud because I believe that the energetic vibrations surrounded me in my house. Even if you don't believe the things you say it is important to say them....such as I am happy. I will find love again. Say whatever you need at the time.

The words begin to take on a life of their own and you begin to change your attitude which causes to you to make more positive choices, thus you keep moving forward on your journey of recovery. It is important to surround yourself with positive people. Those who uplift you, not bring you down. This is a time that you will be creating a new identity for yourself. Everything will be different but you can make it something positive. As the years pass by you can look back and reflect on your strength that brought you to where you are today. Stay strong, it is worth it in the end. I found happiness again so I know it is possible. I have come to the conclusion that we can have more than one soul mate.

Website:
www.recovernowfromloss.com

Twitter:
https://twitter.com/RobinChodak

Facebook:
www.facebook.com/recovernowfromloss

Chapter 12: Grief Lesson Stories - Susan Cowe Miller - Author of Survive And Thrive after Trauma

Emotional Healing practitioner offering help, support and guidance with stress, anxiety and anger issues.

Divorce: Pre and Post-Divorce is my area of expertise and use I use EFT "Tapping" as a basis for my work.

EFT is fast, powerful and effective for any emotional distress.

My Purpose:

My key message: When overcoming trauma or distress you can choose, permit and believe that you can heal: baby steps will take you there.

- to offer hope, inspiration and energy to those wounded by life

– to show that life can change out of all recognition, but for the better.

My Story of Grief:

<u>My husband's death.</u>

I was married for 26 years; happily for many years. The last two years proved very difficult. My husband I accepted was an alcoholic. With much soul searching and angst I accepted I must divorce my husband so that my teenage children and I could live decently and peacefully once again.

Whilst still living at home and having been served divorce papers three weeks previously, my husband died suddenly of a heart attack more or less in front of me and our two children. (I have detailed all of this in my book.)

The first death was the death of my marriage. I closed down emotionally.

The second death was the death of my husband. Very emotionally charged and I was stunned and shocked.

What is the main lesson grief taught you about living?

<u>We only have one life.</u>

We need to make the most of it and do whatever makes us content and fulfilled. When we share our life with others e.g. family - we can still be our own person. We are allowed. No-one can take that power.

As adults, (and bypassing parental responsibilities) I now understand that we cannot be responsible for someone else's behaviour. We are only responsible to ourselves. We should not depend on others to help us on a troubled path. I expect I am saying that we are all alone to a large extent.

I believe that we all have a Life Plan. We just don't know what it is until we are tested by the challenges that slap us around when we least expect it.

How did you come to find acceptance of the loss?

After a few years I intuitively understood a need to deal with the layers of stress I had endured. They could only be detrimental to my health.

I discovered Reiki and EFT/ Matrix Reimprinting.

A search to find meaning and understanding for the crap (Tom use "challenges" if you need a quieter word) was needed.

With deep inner work I had my light bulb moment: I was allowed to live - his time was up.

His time here was complete and my purpose is now to help others manage emotional challenges. To help them feel not so alone.

What advice would you give to someone who has experienced loss recently?

Take it slowly. Time needs to pass before any semblance of normality can once again appear. Find two or three ways to deal with the emotional roller coaster so that in time life can appear fruitful and worth living. Do not have high expectations. Find inner strength.

I promote calm and finding ways to inner peace. Once found that allows confidence and opportunities to consider.

Did anyone say anything to you or do anything for you during your time of grief that really helped you?

My closest friends were supportive. But actually I felt that I was alone. I was responsible for my two teenage children. I had my primary teaching job. I felt safe in my little suit of armour and did not seem able to grieve. But I felt ok. My situation was like some others but unlike so many others. In honesty I felt relief. I had been let off the hook. I use my emotional healing therapies to help me.

A year after the death I had many months of Cruse Counselling. The opportunity to speak about it all, endlessly, did help.

What is your philosophy of grief?

I choose to deserve the many good things life has to offer. (I wish I knew what they will be but feel sure I will know them when they pass my way!) We gain our strength from our biggest challenges. We can free our spirit for good things to once again come our way. We deserve to share and love again. I do not believe that years of self-indulgent mourning is useful.

How has the pain transformed your life in a positive way with how you are now?

When my husband died I was briefly stunned and confused; had some feelings of anger and thoughts that I would never trust again at a deep and intimate level. I had protective armour to keep out *feeling*. I got on with my life and in time allowed myself to relax and to soften my outer layer. The result was I felt vulnerable, needed more counselling and I discovered the world of EFT.

I love helping people who seek a solution to past or recurring negative behaviour; who understand that old memories and beliefs may be unhelpful to them today. I feel fulfilled and so eager to learn more.

I wish to empower others to *Enjoy Life's Journey*.

Writing my book helped me! I was suggesting to others to 'let it go' but I had a thin armour protecting me. So I took off the armour and married my partner of nine years. And that felt good.

Any other lessons you have learnt from grief to share and assist others?

When my husband died it took time to accept that I had been unable to save him. I now realise that I was not responsible: that was a revelation.

I intuitively learned that feelings of e.g. anger, resentment, low self-worth and low self-belief can be overcome. I believe that anger is often a mask for fear, pain or hurt.

We can choose to overcome life's obstacles. Otherwise self-sabotage will reign.

Staying locked in the past is a useless practice. It serves no purpose. We deserve, are worthy and are good enough.

<u>My mother's death.</u>

Recently my mother died aged 87 and that was a different experience. She had lived her life: psychologically her life span was acceptable. I was honoured to be with her when she died but saddened at her passing.

All experiences are deeply personal and individual.

Websites:

http://www.hampshire-eft.co.uk/

http://www.surviveandthriveaftertrauma.com/

Twitter:

https://twitter.com/SusanCowe/

Chapter 13: Grief Lesson Stories - Elizabeth Berrien – The Respite

Hi, I am Elizabeth Berrien. I am the co-founder of The Respite: A Centre for Grief & Hope and the author of *Creative Grieving: A Hip Chick's Path from Loss to Hope.*

Grief Lesson Story

What your site/project purpose is:

My non-profit, The Respite, helps people who are coping with all types of loss. We provide, a safe haven, a supportive community, and take an integrative approach that offers a variety of healing modalities (mind, soul, and body) to empower individuals and families. Our vision is to shift how grief is viewed in the world – moving from shame and isolation to unveiling (or mining) grief's transformative gifts. We welcome grief and provide hope for tomorrow.

My book, *Creative Grieving: A Hip Chick's Path from Loss to Hope*, is my own personal story from loss to hope, and offers creative tips, tools, and resources to help an individual on their grief journey.

Your Story of Grief

My story of loss began in 2008 at the age of twenty-six. After a healthy 9-month pregnancy with my first child, I anticipated an uncomplicated birth. I was young, healthy, and so excited to become a mother and start a family. I had so many hopes and dreams that I had created in my mind and couldn't wait to hold my son in my arms. Tragically, after a fourteen-hour labor, my son was stillborn due to a cord accident. From that moment on, my life was forever changed. I held my son closely and cried as all of my hopes for the future instantly crumbled. I had never known that such a deep pain was possible. I lost a lot of trust and belief in life, and went into a deep depression.

My husband and I both dealt with our grief in our own ways. This created a challenge for us, but we gradually navigated our way through the turmoil we each felt. I eventually became pregnant with our second child and was very nervous throughout the entire pregnancy. I tried to regain some hope and faith in life as I nervously waited for nine months, and was so relieved when our beautiful, healthy daughter was born! Her birth restored some hope in me that life would continue forward and that the worst was now behind us.

My husband at the time was a Special Forces soldier and

owed the military one final deployment before retiring from the service. Brian had to leave for Afghanistan only six months after our daughter was born. He was supposed to be deployed for six months, but was only overseas for six weeks when he was shot and killed while on a mission. Again, I felt the devastating blow of grief. I felt deeply broken and didn't know how I was going to ever move through the pain. I was a twenty-seven year-old widow with a young child and I had never felt more lost in my entire life. I moved to be closer to family and friends who could offer their support and encouragement. In the beginning, I saw only darkness, but as time moved forward and I sought help to cope with my losses, I was gradually able to begin the healing process and see the light again.

What is the main lesson grief taught you about living?

The main lesson that I learned from my grief process has been that we only get one chance at life. It is worth it to take risks for what you believe in and to reach for your dreams because it is important to truly live while you are here! I try to savor the gifts that are in my life today and hold onto what is precious. There isn't a day that goes by without feeling a sense of gratitude in my heart.

How did you come to find acceptance of the loss?

I gradually found acceptance through learning that there are things in life that I simply cannot control. Even though I went through so many feelings that revolved around guilt and shame, I eventually came to the realization that I had done all that I could do in each situation. I had given my all to my loved ones and had done the best that I could. I found peace through the knowledge that I am a human being and that I gave my heart fully.

What advice would you give to someone who has experienced loss recently?

Even though in the beginning it feels as if you will never be able to move forward, get out of bed, laugh, or engage in life again – it DOES get easier. Life will continue to unfold in ways that you might never have imagined. Take it one moment at a time.

There is no "right" way to grieve. You have to do what feels comfortable to you. Try not to put too much pressure on yourself to move through grief quickly as it is a slow process. The healing will take place in its own time.

You don't have to "get over" your loss. You can healthily move through the depths of grief and always remember your loved one! Grieving is a completely normal experience and a part of our journey as a human being. Never apologize for your tears.

Did anyone say anything to you or do anything for you during your time of grief that really helped you?

It was very important to me to have people in my support system that would simply listen. They didn't have to have all of the right words to say. After all, there were no magic words that could "fix" the situation. But it greatly helped to have good listeners as I processed my losses and my feelings. They enabled me to share my heart, which gave me the space to grieve in a way that felt right for me.

What is your philosophy of grief?

I believe that grief is one of our greatest teachers. If we travel the grief journey with an open heart and in search of hope, amazing gifts will come. You can't have darkness without light. Grief has the power to lead one into their greatest calling.

How has the pain transformed your life in a positive way with how you are now?

I have become less fearful in reaching for my goals. Things that once seemed like a distant dream have now become my reality – such as writing a book and starting a non-profit. I have a deeper awareness regarding the things that matter most in life – such as love, family, and friends. I feel joy in a much more profound way when something wonderful happens and I've learned to laugh at myself more. My journey has brought about a deeper sense of self-acceptance and appreciation for who I am and what I'm capable of as a person.

Any other lessons you have learnt from grief to share and assist others?

Grief can lead us to a place of creativity. I encourage anyone grieving to use self-expression and art as a way of coping with the feelings that accompany grief. There are so many ways to release thoughts and feelings – whether through drawing, writing, painting, poetry, journaling, dancing, making music, etc. The possibilities are endless. I think it is important to find something that speaks to your soul so that it may motivate you to make something beautiful out of your experience.

Websites:
http://www.TheRespite.org/
http://www.CreativeGrieving.com/
http://www.SoulWidows.org

Chapter 14: Grief Lesson Stories - Dennis Garcia – Sweet Salutation

Hello, we are a husband and wife duo who have been touched by pregnancy loss. We are looking to share our story in hopes it may provide other couples with support and hope knowing what they are experiencing is normal and there is a light at the end of the tunnel.

Sweet Salutation - Our battle with cervical incompetency and pregnancy loss.

Grief Lesson Story

What our site purpose is.

At Sweet Salutation our mission is to provide a forum for bereaved parents to discuss their thoughts and feelings towards pregnancy loss. Our goal is to eliminate the stigma attached with pregnancy loss by speaking about it, as well to provide a coping mechanism for bereaved parents by creating awareness and initiating dialogue in a safe, warm and welcoming environment.

Sweet Salutation was created to commemorate our two boys Jacob Cody and Zachary Nolan who we've lost due to a physical condition called cervical incompetency. Our boys have made such an impact on our lives in the short time they were here with us. Because we believe that as long as we live, they too shall live; we intend to keep their memory alive by sharing our own stories with pregnancy loss so other families living through similar circumstances may find some comfort in knowing that there are others out there who truly understand and empathize with how they feel. Our site will feature two perspectives of our journey through pregnancy loss. The first through my wife's eyes and the second through mine, with both of us posting our thoughts and feelings with our ongoing battle to overcome cervical incompetency and grow our family.

Your Story of Grief

The first time we heard the term incompetent cervix was the day we lost Jacob on August 21, 2012, after 18 weeks of gestation. Everything leading up to that point was fine, life was good and we had no reason to suspect anything was wrong with the pregnancy. We received regular prenatal care, followed a well balance diet, didn't smoke and/or drink, plus Souky never noticed any miscarriage symptoms like; moderate to heavy bleeding, lower back pain, severe cramping, fever or fatigue.

Other than some morning sickness the pregnancy was going to plan. We were already well into our second trimester and we were reassured even further after receiving positive news on our IPS (Integrated Prenatal Screening) results that ruled out any chromosomal issues. This gave us a false sense of security that we had passed yet another milestone in Jacob's development and our risk of losing him was at its lowest. But sadly, we were wrong and we didn't know at the time but our lives would be changed forever. Without any warning signs my wife's amniotic sac began to funnel out of her while she was in the shower. We rushed to our midwife's office but sadly by late in the evening we had lost Jacob, our first-born angel baby.

Shortly after our loss we began trying again and to our excitement we received another positive pregnancy test in May of 2013. It felt like déjà vu, we did the math and the expected due date would be close to Jacob's, we were going to have another January baby! We were confident the outcome would be different this time around as we were armed with a diagnosis and doctor's referral to the high-risk pregnancy clinic at Hamilton Health Sciences Centre (McMaster University Children's Hospital).

We had a game plan and a team of medical experts who were going to monitor my wife closely for the full duration of the pregnancy. There was never a moment we felt neglected, our medical team answered all our questions and they monitored the pregnancy quite closely. They had us coming in every two weeks for ultrasounds, which we didn't mind so much as we got to see our little guy squirming around at every visit. They also performed all other prenatal tests such as the IPS and urine checks for possible UTIs (urinary tract infections).

Everything was going to plan, and on our 13th week when our baby was considered viable they performed a trans-vaginal cerclage (when successful will prevent the cervix from opening prematurely leading to a preterm birth). Unfortunately, even with medical intervention the cerclage failed and we lost Zachary at 22 weeks and gained our second angel baby.

Our doctor determined that cervical incompetence was the cause of this loss as well. My wife's cervix was too weak and even with the trans-vaginal cerclage, it failed. The problem was the suture was placed too low on her cervix and it needed to be placed much higher. The only way to achieve this was to use a different type of cerclage which would be surgically implanted through the belly. This was called a trans-abdominal cerclage. In order to place this suture at optimal height they would need to perform a small incision through her belly. It would be left there permanently and came along with a higher success rate. Though this information was reassuring, we were still incredibly devastated that we had lost a second baby, we were literally inconsolable.

The weeks following the loss was incredibly difficult, it was like we were surrounded by a dark fog that just wouldn't lift. The majority of our time was spent in bed and we rarely did anything but watch TV, since we had no motivation to do anything at all. If it wasn't for our regular therapist appointments we wouldn't have stepped out of our house. We had a good support system around us, our family, friends, doctors, employer and therapist played such a huge role in our recovery, but, even though they were there for us we had always felt there was something missing.

Through our grieving process, there were many times when we felt isolated and lost. We couldn't really expect everyone to be at our 'beck and call' as we understood they had their own lives and responsibilities to worry about. And although they would be empathetic to us and our situation, they could not fully grasp how we felt inside. To us, we needed to find other people who had walked in our shoes. So we searched online for other families who have gone through similar circumstances and what we found was although there were many other blogs and forums to support mothers through their grieving process, there was very little available for fathers. That's when we came up with an idea to create a blog which discusses both parents' perspective so both parents can find comfort in knowing that the emotional roller coaster they're experiencing is normal, and that their child mattered and was deeply loved.

By sharing our story we hope that other families find solace in knowing that there are others who have walked in their shoes and are still waiting for their rainbow baby, too. Please follow our blog and join us on our journey as we build our family (*biologically, through surrogacy or adoption*), overcome life's obstacles and create our happy ending.

What is the main lesson grief taught you about living?
The main lesson grief has taught us is that, no matter how dark you may find your current situation. If you hang on long enough, you will find the light.

How did you come to find acceptance of the loss?
This was a slow and painful process, but with time and a good

support system behind us we were able to move past this loss. We also realized what we experienced could be shared with other families who have experienced similar circumstances and perhaps provide them with hope in knowing that our journey will go on and we will have our happy ending.

What advice would you give to someone who has experienced loss recently?

Take your time and do not let anyone rush you into anything you don't want to do. Allow yourself to feel the emotions and do not suppress them at all, talk it out with someone you trust. If you feel like the grief is overwhelming, do not feel ashamed to use any of the resources available to you, such as: psychological and/ or therapeutic counselling, medication and/or joining a support group.

Did anyone say anything to you or do anything for you during your time of grief that really helped you?

Our therapist once said, "Losing someone you love is like losing a limb. You will need to learn how to live without it, you will never be the same and it will be difficult at first but eventually you will get there."

What is your philosophy of grief?

Surviving grief is inevitable, we will all get there one day. The experiences we have in life is what builds us, surviving grief will only make you a stronger person.

How has the pain transformed your life in a positive way with how you are now?

I believe experiencing such profound grief has increased our level of compassion. We want to help other bereaved parents overcome their grief through sharing our own stories, as well as creating a warm and welcoming environment on our forums page for everyone to discuss pregnancy loss related topics.

We also would like to adopt a child from an orphanage somewhere in Asia. Our goal as husband and wife is to grow our family, and we won't allow the obstacles in our way from slowing us down. We want to make as big an impact in our child's life as possible. We feel we can achieve this by rescuing an abandoned child in a third world country. As boys are more prized in the Orient, we would prefer to adopt a daughter where her talents can shine and her potential can be limitless if given a chance to grow up in Canada. We have set up a donation page on our website and if anybody would like to help us realize our dream of building our family, visit our website: www.sweetsalutation.com/ and please donate. Even a single dollar can go a long way to making our dream a reality.

Any other lessons you have learnt from grief you'd like to share?

If life gives you lemons, make lemonade.

Website:

http://*sweetsalutation.com/*

Chapter 15: Grief Lesson Stories - Kathy - Greet Grief

Grief Lesson Story

What your site/project purpose is:

My first intention in writing a blog was for the sole purpose of writing down my stories. To have a place where they would be brought to life and where my family would be able to access them. Then I realized that my experiences and the lessons that I had learned from journeying through grief, might serve as examples to others of how to navigate through this time of darkness.

I hope that my site can be a resource to others because I feel we have little education regarding the topic of loss/grief. I hope that those who read my stories do not hear just the pain and suffering, but they see the potential for healing in their own lives and the hope of better tomorrows.

Your Story of Grief

On February 13, 1990 my husband went to work and never came home. He was 36 years old and died from a head injury at the work site after falling from a second story roof. I was called by his co-worker and told to come to the hospital, not knowing that he had died immediately, the paramedics were not able to revive him.

As an R.N., I was planning for what might be as I drove to the hospital, but NOTHING prepared me for becoming a 29-year-old widow and a single parent of my 2-year-old son.

What is the main lesson grief taught you about living?

That death is a part of living. That we all experience it ourselves and will experience the death of those we love throughout our life. But death is only one aspect of living. When the worst thing happens you now have that experience, so you can live more fully, holding nothing back because you know life here on earth is fragile and finite.

How did you come to find acceptance of the loss?

I think acceptance is an interesting word - on one hand, I still don't accept that my husband had to die so young, and that he misses the joys of this life, especially getting to see his son's accomplishments. But, I got through the initial shock and disbelief one hour and one day at a time, by doing my work! By experiencing whatever feelings/issues came up and not being afraid to express what was in my heart. Even if that meant being angry (at God, those who still had their husbands, at his company), or afraid or extremely sad. I also learned how to "accept" my new self - the one who was muddling through in the unique way that was mine!

What advice would you give to someone who has experienced loss recently?

I have run grief support groups for years and my very first piece of advice is - "Self-care, even if you don't know how to do it, is mandatory NOW." Take care of your body - eating, small frequent healthy snacks even if you have to force yourself, getting exercise so that you might be able to sleep at night. Don't think that numbing yourself with alcohol or drugs will help, it just prolongs the healing.

Take care of your mind and spirit - if you are an artist, force yourself to draw, if you are a dancer, get up and dance. If you are outraged, get gloves and a punching bag and scream. Read books that describe what "normal" grief is so it will validate your feelings. Attend a support group, but give it more than one time and know that it is hard to hear other people's stories. It will get easier and the support is priceless. Don't be afraid to find a good therapist, and don't be afraid to look again if the first one isn't a good fit. Journal, meditate, read, pray and avoid people who "just don't get it!"

Did anyone say anything to you or do anything for you during your time of grief that really helped you?

The simplest things seemed to mean the most - my neighbour left her light on as a sign that they were there, even in the middle of the night.

My husband's friends made sure that everything in the house was working - came to fix a leaky sink, shovel snow, etc. The people who were the most helpful gave me specific times/dates for example: "I would like to pick your son up for a play date on _____ at _____ time, is that okay?" Those grieving are exhausted and if you say "call me if you need anything, they never will!" So call ahead and tell them when you are coming and what you will be doing! "I would like to bring dinner for you and stay with you to eat it."

Another gift that I was given is that my closest and most helpful family and friends, talked about my husband Chris and to use his name around me. We reminisced and they were NOT afraid of my tears, they shared theirs also!

What is your philosophy of grief?

Grief is one of the hardest things I have ever had to deal with; however, it taught me a lot about myself. It also showed me who was able to walk through it all with me and the people who weren't capable of it. It taught me invaluable lessons that have helped me through subsequent losses, even those that didn't involve death.

How has the pain transformed your life in a positive way with how you are now?

Learning as much as I could about this process over the last 23 years, I am now able to help others. I have developed bereavement care programs within area churches, ageing communities and have taught many classes about grief and loss. I have been a support group facilitator for 20 years and now with my blog and Facebook page, I hope to continue to offer hope and healing.

Any other lessons you have learnt from grief to share and assist others?

Well-meaning family and friends will try to protect you in their desire to help. Their pain for you is great, but don't let them take over your life even if that feels like the easiest way through. Find inner strength by listening closely to your intuition - your gut will lead you to what is right for YOU. Each path is unique, do it in your time and in your way!

Website:

http://greetgrief.com/

Twitter:

https://twitter.com/greet_grief

Facebook:

www.facebook.com/GreetGrief

Chapter 16: Grief Lesson Stories - Kate Hamilton - Funeral Friend/Mourning Cross

Grief Lesson Story

Introduction

My name is Kate Hamilton and I live with my husband, mum and dog in Ireland, on the border between Belfast and Dublin. I have spent over 15 years working for charitable organisations in areas of highest deprivation and political unrest as a community worker. I have always been interested in running my own business without really knowing what that business would be. Never in a million years did I ever think that I would end up working in the area of grief, or the funeral industry. I certainly did not expect that our family would revive an old tradition and develop the Mourning Cross bereavement pins, nor did I think I would start writing a blog about all things death and funerals, or study End of Life Coaching given the losses we have experienced in our family. I now believe that my life and loss experiences have led me here like so many others who have ended up working in this field.

My Site:

Our business is Mourning Cross, we provide bereavement pins that are worn by the immediate family of the deceased to identify them to attendees at wakes and funerals. The idea was borne from a conversation between my sisters and mum, my sister who had been to a wake of her friend's grandmother explained how uncomfortable and embarrassed she felt as a result of not being able to locate her friend who was not in the wake house at the time, and not knowing the immediate family with whom she should sympathise. Each of us gave examples of wakes and funerals that we had attended where we had experienced similar, uncomfortable and embarrassing situations. We also recalled our own family wake of my father and how some visitors had walked past us not realizing that we were daughters and how uncomfortable that felt. We talked about the loud whispers of people asking who was who and the stories that are lost about the deceased as a result of missed opportunities for sharing.

As a result of our own experience we designed and developed the Mourning Cross and non-denominational circle bereavement pins which are presented on a card with the poem entitled "It's My Time" by Angel Lady Jackie Newcomb. We also found out that we are actually reviving the old and lost tradition of wearing black arm bands that identified the grieving. We believe that reviving and preserving this tradition provides a symbolic and special significance in remembering the departed and respecting the grieving at what is a very difficult time. We are passionate in reviving this old tradition using a respectful symbol to enhance the funeral experience not only for attendees but for the families of the deceased who benefit from the wonderful stories that would have been lost. Families love them and some people wear the bereavement pins as an outward expression of grief and respect daily and on Anniversaries.

I have also started a blog, a go-to resource that provides information and support to families when making funeral arrangements. I have been fortunate in connecting with some really experienced grief support specialists in the field who have contributed excellent articles to help support families after a loss. I try and update the blog regularly and have now achieved over 10,000 visitors per month.

Your Personal Experience of Grief

Death has been a feature of our lives from a very young age. My father took us to funerals of his uncles and aunts, I remember not wanting to be there, and it was not a good experience. The sense of sadness, not to mention seeing a corpse was very frightening.

My first experience of a traumatic loss was when I was 17, my friend and I were spinning around in her car when we met her cousin Turlough on the road. He was going to collect his grandmother and brother to take them to evening Mass. We pulled alongside his car and spoke to him confirming that we would meet him in the nightclub later that evening. We said goodbye and drove to our local town. Whilst travelling on the main road, we came upon a car accident, we could see that it was serious and without hesitation drove to the nearest garage to phone for an ambulance and fire brigade. We were very shaken and decided to just sit for a while before going home. My friend dropped me off to my house where my father was waiting for us. He told my friend to go home straight away, my heart dropped, I knew it was bad news. He sat me down and told me what had happened. Turlough whom we had been speaking to only an hour before, was killed in that accident. His grandmother and brother survived the accident but he was killed on impact. The accident was a head-on collision, the driver of the other car was not familiar with the road. We were absolutely devastated; Turlough was only 17 years old. We had lost school friends before in primary and secondary school but this was different, we had spent our whole lives together and his death changed me forever. Two weeks later my grandfather whom I adored also died very suddenly from a heart attack at 67.

Over the years our family has experienced many tragedies including an aunt whose car exploded in a car accident, two uncles that died from heart attacks at 45 and 47, my father, who died 20 years ago from throat cancer at 53, another aunt who was 47 and died from cancer, two of my friends were killed in separate road accidents. Two of my friends died from suicide and I have lost many others including work colleagues. If I were to count all of the funerals I have attended over my 44 years on this earth, I am sure that it would be in the hundreds. There came a point that I just said, no, I just can't go to another funeral.

What is the main lesson grief taught you about living?

I remember on the day of father's funeral, my grandmother was 87 years old at the time and before she went home she gently said to us girls; "Grieve, but not for too long." I was 24 at the time and remember feeling a sense of wonder at her statement and thinking to myself; "how could she say that about her son and our father" and at that time. I felt angry, I didn't understand how she could make such a comment and particularly on the day of my father's funeral. A few years later during a chat with someone, I remember a comment made which me reminded me of what my grandmother had told us "Grieve but not for too long." I pondered on what my grandmother had said and realised that, not only was she correct in her statement, but she was also qualified to make it given the devastating tragedies she had experienced in her life. She had grieved all of her life and didn't want us to suffer in the same way.

How did you come to find acceptance of the loss?

The final turning point that allowed me to let go and live again was a poem. My husband had bought me an angel book by

Author and Poet Jacky Newcomb, on the front page was the poem, "It's My Time". As I read it, my heart filled with sorrow and pain but then turned to a sense of relief. I started to cry, I remember making the decision that day, "to let go of grief." I had grieved enough. I had started researching, looking for answers to so many questions; "where are they? can we communicate with them?" and I haven't stopped researching since.

I started down a road of Spirituality, learning about God and the Angels and reading everything spiritual. I have asked many questions and because I am now open to listening and seeing, I feel that I get signs. For example, just before Christmas I asked God for a sign that everything would be alright regarding a certain situation and I asked for a sign. My little dog was fussing at a window and when I went over to the window, a beautiful butterfly was flapping its wings trying to get out. As everyone knows, butterflies are very rarely seen in December. I truly believe it was and is a sign.

I have learned that we have a short time on this planet. We have one life and we are all going to die. It's the normal and natural life cycle, it is also normal and natural to grieve but there comes a time when you have to replace grief with missing and not allow your loss to consume your life. Life will be different, but it's not over. You must live until you die and try, as hard as it is, to find happiness. You don't know how long you will be here. My father used to say, "There'll not be a word about us in 100 years." I started appreciating all of the memories I had been lucky enough to make with those who are no longer here. Appreciation and prayer are powerful supports.

What advice would you give to someone who has experienced loss recently?

Be gentle with yourself, take time to grieve. Talk to close family and friends and share memories, cry, laugh, and Pray to God and the Angels to help you, minute by minute, hour by hour. Take one day at a time, yes it's an old cliché but we shouldn't underestimate the wisdom of those. Ask yourself, "What would your loved one say to you right now? What would they want you to do right now? I know they would want you to live your life with them in your heart, free from guilt, anger, pain, sorrow. They would want you to be HAPPY. They would want you to "Grieve, but not for too long." Don't put yourself through the what ifs, what if we had done this, or that. Understand that your loved one's path was their path, "not yours."

Did anyone say anything to you or do anything for you during your time of grief that really helped you?

I now understand that there are no words of comfort, either given or offered immediately following a loss. Most people are in shock and denial especially in the first few months. As well-meaning as people are, and they are well meaning, grief is a very individual experience, no two people grieve in the same way, and that is important to remember. When my father died my grandmother's comment, "Grieve but not for too long," seemed a ridiculous thing to say and her comment was completely overshadowed by the immense pain, emotional and our physical exhaustion. We had nursed my father at home for a long time before he died. We had spent months travelling to hospitals and we were really exhausted.

I do remember the stories that people told us about my father, how comforting and wonderful that people thought so much of him and I can honestly say that we found out so much about him that we hadn't known. That is why we would love if people would share their relationship and experience of knowing the deceased, i.e. instead of saying I'm so sorry etc. Tell the family what their loved one meant to you and leave them with a story if you can.

What is your philosophy of grief?

My spirituality has changed my philosophy on grief and death and has given me a better understanding that when someone you love dies whatever the circumstances and age, "It's their time." As hard as it is, and as long as it takes to accept death, whatever the circumstance even suicide, I have learned the importance of living, not to forget, not to stop missing, being sad from time to time, but to accept and live my life each day. We are all heading the same way, in the words of my father; *"You don't know the minute or hour that you could go."* I now honour their lives by enjoying my life and I try to choose happiness. I don't think I will ever stop missing them.

I have written and received many articles which are available to read on our funeral friend.co.uk website.

How has the pain transformed your life in a positive way with how you are now?

I think working for a charitable organisation in areas of high deprivation and political unrest helped me over the years, and in part, the losses. When you see what others have experienced, you realise that no matter how much pain and grief you are experiencing, others have so much more. When you list all of the people and things you are grateful for in your life, somehow it helps change what you are focusing on. If I feel myself getting sad e.g. on New Year's Eve, I acknowledge those I miss and feel happy and grateful for those still with me and enjoy myself.

When I go to a wake or funeral, I now just hold the hand of the family member and say something nice about them. We in Ireland say "I am sorry for your loss." It's just a cultural way of expressing sympathy when there are no other words.

Any other lessons you have learnt from grief to share and assist others?

– Grieve but not for too long

I have learned that I did grieve for too long. I couldn't let go and missed many years of living life to the full. Remember there can be a happy life on the other side of grief, life will be different but it can be meaningful. I know people who live their life in constant grief and self- pity. What a waste of the short time they have on this earth. It's your choice how long you grieve. I remember the day I decided that I needed to let go, I felt that a weight had been lifted. I felt happy, and a knowing that it is alright to live your life, to laugh, have fun and enjoy yourself.

– Pray

Ask God for help, whether you believe in a higher source or not, no matter how angry you may feel, try it. Take time to be still and ask God and your loved one for help through the pain, anger, loss, sleeplessness, depression, loneliness, hurt, and all of the other emotions you will experience minute by minute, hour by hour and take one day at a time. Each morning ask God to help you to-day and each night thank him for your day.

I found the Serenity prayer very comforting:
- God grant me the serenity to accept the things I cannot change;
- Courage to change the things I can;
- And wisdom to know the difference.
- Living one day at a time;
- Enjoying one moment at a time;
- Accepting hardships as the pathway to peace;
- Taking, as He did, this sinful world as it is, not as I would have it;
- Trusting that He will make all things right if I surrender to His Will;
- That I may be reasonably happy in this life and supremely happy with Him
- Forever in the next. Amen.

– Cry

Crying is part and parcel of the grieving process. You may experience a wave of grief from time to time, sometimes we experience triggers that catch us unaware. You may hear a song, a smell, etc. Crying releases the emotion of grief and was very important for me.

– Be gentle with yourself

Look after your health. I didn't, I lost weight and ended up very ill myself. Don't take any type of stimulants e.g. alcohol or sleeping tablets. You may numb the pain for a short time but you can't avoid the pain and you certainly don't want to become addicted to any depressants.

- Forgive

Forgive the "do gooders, nosy parkers, ignorant people," those people who make totally inappropriate comments, "They know not what they do." If you can remember this, you will save yourself the added annoyance and in my experience anger. Some people are totally clueless and seem as if they have not got a compassionate bone in their body. Make an excuse in your head for their comments or behaviour and never give any credence to them.

- Life Changing Decisions

It is true when people advise not to make any life changing decisions in the first few years of a loss. Some people want to move house, jobs etc. You may feel that you should just run away from everything that reminds you of your loss. Unfortunately it doesn't help ease the pain, or change the process of grieving.

As mentioned before, I have more articles and tips on dealing with grief on the funeralfriend blog.

Websites:

www.mourningcross.com
www.funeralfriend.co.uk

Twitter:

https://twitter.com/mourningcross

Chapter 17: Grief Lesson Stories - Kimberly Rinaldi – Live-Joy-Fully

Grief Lesson Stories

What your site/project purpose is:

My name is Kimberly Rinaldi and I teach Lessons in Joyful Living.

I believe happiness is overrated and that we are called to Live-Joy-Fully. Joy comes from within and it truly is the peace of knowing it is a choice you can make at any time.

I help people understand that every experience is a neutral until you place a value on it and the good news is you can go back and revalue any experience, if you are willing to.

Your Story of Grief

I was 39 years old when I had my first loss. It was my father. We had been fighting for his life for more than 10 years as he battled complications from diabetes, cardiac events, leukemia and congestive heart failure. I felt like I spent those years in a constant state of fear and grief.

When he had a hemorrhagic stroke and was pronounced brain dead I was the one to take the lead and make the tough decisions.

The thing was he and I had already discussed it several times. He asked me to make the tough decision, he said; "Your mom won't and your sister can't, please don't leave me on life support." I agreed.

His next statement was always, "Don't be angry with your sister, she can't be there, she won't be there." I would smile and say, "Of course I won't be angry, we all have to handle this the way we need to."

Full on lying through my teeth. You see, I was the one who went with him to his oncology, cardiology and lab appointments. I figured the least my sister could do was be there for him when he passed. I LIED because I knew for sure I'd be mad as hell if she left.

As it turned out, we were all there when he was taken off life support. Yes, I made the decision. My mom wouldn't and my sister couldn't. At 1:11pm my sister turned to me and broke down, she asked me not to be angry. She begged me to let her leave, she couldn't be there when he drew his last breath. It was too hard for her. I knew that moment he was right, she was right. I hugged her and told her to go. I knew he had been waiting for her to leave. And at 1:16pm he passed. Peacefully and on his terms.

What is the main lesson grief taught you about living?

It's only too late to change the day after you're dead. And there is joy to be found in the most peculiar places, even in grief.

How did you come to find acceptance of the loss?

I came to see that all things are as they should be. The synchronicities surrounding his passing were too blatant to miss.

Dad asked to have "Happy Trails to You" played at his funeral. He worked at the same hospital Roy Rogers and Dale Evans both passed away at and they had been childhood heroes to him. He died on the anniversary of Roy Rogers' death. I went to the florist and asked for a floral horseshoe with "Happy Trails to You" on the ribbon, the florist walked away (I thought I had offended him, this was after all for a funeral.) He returned with a photo album of his childhood, his grandfather worked for Roy and Dale (mind you this florist was 119 miles away from the high desert area where Dad died.) "Happy Trails" is not a song you hear very often, I heard it 20+ times over the next two weeks EVERYWHERE I went as did everyone who was with me.

What advice would you give to someone who has experienced loss recently?

Grieve, don't let anyone tell you how to or how long to, this is your time to heal. You will know when it's time to move forward, not on; but forward.

Did anyone say anything to you or do anything for you during your time of grief that really helped you?

My father and I planned his funeral, we discussed everything about his passing. I knew what he wanted and what was going to be. As a medium I also got to work with him for 5 years after his death, but that dear friends is another story.

What is your philosophy of grief?

It is the pain of the illusion of separation. Where ever you are when you think of a departed loved one that is where they are. Know this.

How has the pain transformed your life in a positive way with how you are now?

I understand that we have an expiration date, each of us. And each day we live puts us that much closer. There is so much for us to do, to learn, to share. Time is the only real currency we have, I've learned not to waste it.

Any other lessons you have learnt from grief to share and assist others?

We shared this poem at Dad's funeral:

Do not stand at my grave and weep
I am not there. I do not sleep.
I am a thousand winds that blow.
I am the diamond glints on snow.
I am the sunlight on ripened grain.
I am the gentle autumn rain.
When you awaken in the morning's hush
I am the swift uplifting rush

Of quiet birds in circled flight.
I am the soft stars that shine at night.
Do not stand at my grave and cry;
I am not there. I did not die.

—Mary Elizabeth Frye

Website:

www.KimberlyRinaldi.com

Twitter:

twitter.com/Live_Joy_Fully

Chapter 18: Grief Lesson Stories - Elke Barber – Is Daddy Coming Back In A Minute

Grief Lesson Story

Introduction

Hi, my name is Elke Barber. I am a children's book author, having written and self-published a fully-illustrated picture book explaining sudden death to very young children in words they can understand in December 2012. It has just been nominated for the prestigious CILIP Carnegie and Kate Greenaway children's book award. My second book *What Happened to Daddy's Body?* is due to be self-published in 2014, and explains to very young children what happens after death - cremation and burial, and it shows the reader, in pictures and in words, what we chose to do with my late husband's ashes.

I am a young widow, aged 34, a mum of two young kids, who were 11 months and 3 years when their Daddy died, now a step-mum to a further five.

In 2012 I was diagnosed with, and fought, a very aggressive breast cancer, aged only 37.

What your site/project purpose is:

I am passionate about helping very young bereaved children and their families/carers. There is currently no help available for children under four, that I am aware of, and only very few child-friendly picture books explaining death. *Is Daddy Coming Back in a Minute?* and *What Happened to Daddy's Body?* will help give you the words, the confidence and the strength to explain what has happened when a young child has been bereaved. It will further help the child understand that they are not alone, and that there is nothing to be ashamed of. From experience, I know that, to a young child, there is no difference between asking, "How does an aeroplane stay in the air?" and "What happened to Daddy's body?" I believe passionately in being honest with children, and explaining in words and pictures they can understand.

Your Story of Grief

I was widowed, very suddenly and unexpectedly, in April 2009, aged only 34. My husband and our three-year-old son had gone to a static caravan in the Lake District (we live in Scotland), for a father/son bonding weekend. On the day they were due to return, I received a phone call, explaining that my husband had been taken seriously ill. I didn't understand, as I had only spoken to him a couple of hours earlier, and everything seemed fine. What I didn't know was that, at that point in time, he had already died from a massive heart attack. Alex, our three-year-old son, had been the only person with him, and had somehow managed to get help and an ambulance to the caravan. Martin died at the scene, also aged only 34. There was no family history, and he had suffered no previous symptoms. He died only four days before our daughter's first birthday. It was now up to me to travel the 160 miles to the Lake District to explain to our son that his Daddy was never coming back. Our book, *Is Daddy Coming Back in a Minute?* is based on my explanation at the time, and the relentless questions by Alex that followed. It is written from his, a three-year-old's, point of view, in his own words.

Less than three years later, just when I thought I had pieced my life back together, I was diagnosed with an aggressive form of breast cancer. My children were now only three and six, with Olivia being only a month older than Alex was when their Daddy died. I panicked. Then I fought. I had 6 rounds of chemotherapy over nearly 5 months, then surgery and extensive radiotherapy. I am still on hormone treatment, and will remain on that for another 8 1/2 years.

What is the main lesson grief taught you about living?

Buddha supposedly once said "The trouble is, you think you have time." That quote struck a chord with me. I think we are all guilty of saying or thinking things like, "We'll do that when the kids are a bit bigger/we have a bit more money/the mortgage is paid off/we are retired".....

I was a person who thought they already had their work/life balance right, and I thought I was already enjoying the little things, like a cuddle from my children, making cupcakes and jumping in puddles. And I did. Yet, both the sudden death of my husband, and even more so, my own cancer diagnosis, made me understand that it is not just about all the people "I look after," it is also about me. I learnt that it is okay to look after yourself. That I count just as much as everybody else. That it is okay to ask for help. That it is okay to be sad, but it is also okay to be happy. That you can feel intense grief and joy, all at the same time.

I learnt that guilt is one of the most useless and unhelpful emotions there are. I was lucky, in that when Martin died, I could say that I had no regrets. Wouldn't do anything differently. There was nothing I wish I had said or done. And I still live by that. I tell the people I love that I love them. And I don't just tell them. I hug them, I enjoy life with them, and I am there for them. Whether that means sitting up chatting until 3am, or jumping in puddles with the kids. I am not afraid to be silly in public. Not scared to do crazy things. I jump off cliffs, and float down rivers just wearing a wet suit, and I feel so alive. I cherish every moment, and I am beginning to understand that everything in life is just a phase. It will change. Good or bad. Enjoy every minute. And don't be a victim. Yes, bad things do happen, but it is how you deal with them that will set you apart. Focus on the good; and believe me, there always is something good. Sometimes it just takes a while to see it.

When I was diagnosed with my cancer, all I could think was how lucky I was to have found it when I did. I was lucky to be able to have treatment. And I am very lucky to still be here. I have learnt to always follow my gut feeling. Trust it. It is always right.

How did you come to find acceptance of the loss?

I guess that depends on your understanding of the word "acceptance." Do I shrug my shoulders and say, "It's okay that he's died"? No, because it's not. And it never will be. But I have understood that there is nothing I can do about it. I can't sit in a dark room for three years and bring him back, for example. Death always comes too soon, and it is always a terrible, life-changing event for the people who are left. But am I grateful for everything we had? Yes. And have I changed for having had him in my life? Definitely. Do we still talk about him? All the time. How did I do that? I am not sure. I guess I was determined to make the best out of everything, for the kids, for us, and because he never got the chance. I feel strongly that it is up to me to show my children that it is okay to be sad, but it's also okay to be happy. To give them ways of coping with their grief and with life, and to be emotionally intelligent and caring. When Alex says that he doesn't want to be happy, because he feels that "Daddy is missing out," I stop what I am doing, give him a big hug, and tell him that he's right; Daddy IS missing out. But that doesn't mean that we shouldn't be happy. Some things we can't change. Those we need to accept. As for the rest? Well, sometimes we just need to adjust the way we think about them.

What advice would you give to someone who has experienced loss recently?

I know it sounds like a cliché, but it WILL get easier. Keep talking. There are forums online, or see a counsellor. If you don't like the first one, see a different one. Talk to your friends, your family, even your Facebook friends. You have every right to feel upset, but please don't be a victim. The person who will suffer most if you are is you. Try and change your way of thinking. Believe me, I know sometimes it's not easy; but I believe it's the only way. Keep moving. Baby steps. Little goals. Be kind to yourself. Don't feel guilty. It wasn't your fault.

Did anyone say anything to you or do anything for you during your time of grief that really helped you?

To be honest, it was the little practical things that helped the most, but I suspect that is because I had very young children. The friend who picked them up from nursery, mowed our lawn, or cooked the kids'tea. The girlfriend who came over with a bottle of fizzy wine, some bath bombs and some edible stars. The friends who understood I couldn't go out at night, so they got a babysitter instead and came over for take-away. The friends who never got bored of listening, even when I ranted on about the same thing they had already listened to a million times.

What is your philosophy of grief?

I believe grief is a part of you - you can't fight it; you just have to go with it. Feel it. Be sad. Be angry. Cry, kick, walk, and talk. But don't give up. Keep moving. Keep dreaming, and don't feel guilty for feeling happy; glimpses at first, then more intense happiness. It's okay. You don't have to punish yourself on top of already grieving. We all know you are sad. We all want you to be happy. You deserve to be happy.

How has the pain transformed your life in a positive way with how you are now?

Like I said earlier, I already enjoyed and was grateful for the little things in life and spoke my mind. But the main difference now is that I don't put things I dream about off any more. If I can do them, I will. I have booked and been on that holiday that I thought I couldn't have because of kids or money or stuff, and it was one of the best things ever. I have been to the cinema, climbed trees, and jumped off cliffs into icy cold rivers. With the help of my wonderful crowdfunding supporters, I have self-published my first book, and getting feedback from the families and children has helped and been absolutely overwhelming. I have stopped beating myself up for "not being good enough" and "not doing enough," and have started to really focus on all the things I have done and am doing. I won't lie, some days I struggle. But I always get up again and fight.

Any other lessons you have learnt from grief to share and assist others?

Be yourself. Follow your dreams. Don't give up. Be kind to yourself, and to others. It's okay to be sad, but it's okay to be happy too. Be happy. YOU are the only person who can make you happy. Sometimes that means adjusting your way of thinking. Try. It gets easier. Big hugs, from one survivor to another. XXX.

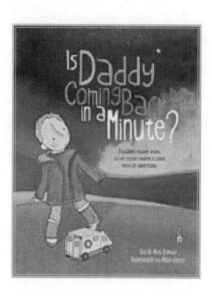

Website:

www.isdaddycomingbackinaminute.com

Twitter:

twitter.com/missingdaddy

Chapter 19: Grief Lesson Stories - Hilary Robinson – The Copper Tree

Grief Lesson Story

What your site/project/book purpose is:

I am the author of a picture book, *The Copper Tree*, written for young children, and their carers, to help guide them through the experience of bereavement and grief. The approach is one of accessibility in that it is narrated from the point of view of a child, Olivia. At all times during the development of the text and the illustrations we took advice from bereavement specialists, child care professionals as well as bereaved families.

Your Story of Grief

My sister in law, Caroline, was a much loved teacher when she developed breast cancer at the age of 32. She lived with the disease for 7 years. In order to help my own then young daughters I wrote a story about a young teacher who becomes ill and then dies. The story was designed to help them cope with what had happened.

What is the main lesson grief taught you about living?

We discovered that children benefit from a sensitive, direct approach. Language was a key point of focus. To say to a child that we've "lost" someone, to them, means, in their minds, they may be found again. We also found that young children don't understand why they are feeling the way they do and often their behaviour may be affected. This is quite normal. But if children can understand why they feel like they do it may then help them come to terms with what has happened. So in short, my grief experience, the therapeutic nature of writing, which is what comes most naturally to me, has helped me in terms of the tools needed to help others.

How did you come to find acceptance of the loss?

I came to understand that Caroline's legacy was a living reminder of her life. That everything she had taught, shared, enjoyed, was part of me and our family and those whose lives she touched. That would continue whenever we shared those experiences with others. So she was, and is, living on in many ways whether that be the child she taught to write, the child she helped with a problem, or even the careful way she crafted her own Easter cards during the last year of her life, despite finding a pen difficult to hold.

What advice would you give to someone who has experienced loss recently?

I think it's important to understand the main stages of grief, and that it's natural to be in shock, to be sad, to be angry and I think it is also important to share how you feel with those most experienced in dealing with such problems. Rationalising an emotion is one of the best ways of being able to process it. A problem shared really is a problem halved, providing it is shared with someone qualified or experienced enough to help.

Did anyone say anything to you or do anything for you during your time of grief that really helped you?

C. S. Lewis's book, *A Grief Observed* starts with the line "Grief feels just like fear" and it does. I realised that everyone feels the same way and I also realised that far from being a cliché "time" is indeed a great healer. But it does take time.

What is your philosophy of grief?

That it is a necessary and essential part of bereavement, and that it is better to have loved and lost than never to have loved at all.

How has the pain transformed your life in a positive way with how you are now?

I would like to think that all life's challenging experiences have enabled me to empathise with others in similar situations. I think to some extent as Caroline had been ill for so long we knew that her life would be cut short and to some extent we had come to accept that but it was still a shock when she finally died. The ensuing grief was just as tortuous but it gave me the creative energy to produce something positive for the benefit of others.

Any other lessons you have learnt from grief to share and assist others?

To be aware that there could be a trigger for emotion at any time and sometimes when you least expect it. But that is quite natural, as is life, as is death.

The Copper Tree – Hilary Robinson

Website:

www.hilaryrobinson.co.uk

Twitter:

twitter.com/H_A_Robinson

Chapter 20: Grief Lesson Stories - Litsa Williams and Eleanor Haley - What's Your Grief

Grief Lesson Story

What your site/project purpose is:

Aside from being mental health professionals with 10+ years of experience in grief and bereavement, we have both experienced the death of a parent and know what it's like to deal with life after loss. We experienced grief in our twenties and at that time neither of us knew what resources were available to us. We fumbled through the darkness alone, unable to find outlets that resonated with us, and surrounded by people who didn't understand what we were going through.

When we set out to create "What's Your Grief" we committed ourselves to providing a realistic picture of grief and to explore coping skills for anyone and everyone, regardless of their unique strengths and weaknesses. Specifically, our mission is to promote grief education, exploration, and expression in both practical and creative ways through

- Education that reaches beyond generalization
- Practical and specific suggestions for moving forward
- Modes of self-exploration and self-expression that suit all types of thinkers and doers
- Ways to honor and remember deceased loved ones
- A supportive community

Your Story of Grief

Eleanor: My mother died at the age of 57 almost one year after being diagnosed with Pancreatic Cancer. I was 24 so just on the verge of being an actual, real adult. I often wonder what it would be like to still have my mother; as a wife, mother, and professional, I have come upon many a bridge I wish she were here to walk across with me.

Litsa: My father died when I was 18 years old, the summer after my freshman year of college. Though he was diagnosed with a blood and bone marrow disorder that we knew could be terminal, things unfolded very quickly when he developed an infection. Until just a week before his death we were still hopeful he could recover. In the 5 years that followed his death I lost both my grandmothers, my great-uncle, and my sister's boyfriend (who was like a member of our family). I became acutely aware of the impact of grief not just on individuals, but on families as a whole, and the many different ways that people cope with loss.

What is the main lesson grief taught you about living?

Eleanor: Grief has taught me that there is something to be learned from even the worst and most painful circumstances. There is also usually something to laugh at.

Litsa: Grief has taught me to keep things in perspective. When you lose people who mean so much to you, you quickly realize what is truly valuable in life. Grief may be the worst thing you ever experience, but it can make you a better person.

How did you come to find acceptance of the loss?

Eleanor: I found acceptance after I transitioned through denial, anger, bargaining, and depression. Just kidding. I guess, because my mother was terminally ill for a year, I started to accept the loss before she even died. Nothing humbles your sense of control more than watching cancer take over your loved one's body.

Litsa: So, this question is a tough one for me, because I hate the word "acceptance." I am a very rational and analytical personal and, hence, a very rational and analytical griever. In many ways I found a deep acceptance of the loss almost immediately. That being said, almost 15 years later I continue to believe that acceptance is a bit of a myth. There are still days that some new and exciting thing happens in my life and I face the reality, all over again, that my dad won't be here for it. I think we go through reacceptance forever (or, at least I do).

What advice would you give to someone who has experienced loss recently?

Eleanor: Understand that you will feel a vast range of emotions at varying times. There is no "normal," so don't feel crazy when your grief doesn't follow some pattern or look the way it does on TV.

Litsa: 1) Don't let others tell you how to grieve. 2) See a counselor – a little counselling never hurt anyone! 3) Grief brings out the best and worst in families, so be prepared that it can be a roller coaster.

Did anyone say anything to you or do anything for you during your time of grief that really helped you?

Eleanor: I appreciated the people who recognized I am a private person and didn't push me to act, feel, or talk a certain way. I also appreciated those people who were able to laugh and remember the good times despite the sadness.

Litsa: I appreciated anyone who was willing to talk about my dad and share memories. Also, I had a professor who learned about my dad and he gave me a book of poetry by a woman about the death of her father. I don't know why it stuck with me more than almost anything else – I didn't even like the poetry that much. I think it was that it acknowledged that he recognized the impact this loss would have on me, maybe even more than I did. The book was by Sharon Olds, *The Father*.

What is your philosophy of grief?

Eleanor: Honestly I don't think I have a philosophy. Grief is complicated and dynamic. It's difficult to pin down.

Litsa: Can I steal Eleanor's answer?? I don't have a single philosophy about grief and I have a Master's Degree in philosophy - you would think if anyone would have developed a grief philosophy, I would have! I think grief is so individual, so complex, and exists forever in so many changing forms that it doesn't have any one "essence." I don't think it can be boiled down in a way that wouldn't do a disservice to grievers.

How has the pain transformed your life in a positive way with how you are now?

Eleanor: I think it's caused me to value the relationships I have more than I did before. Perhaps this is also because I've matured, but I think it's brought me closer to my dad and my siblings. Also I cherish every moment I have with my daughters because I know how precious they are.

Litsa: Grief has helped me keep life in perspective. I think it helps me value the things that are really important, and let the other crap go. It has inspired me to make sure that I always feel like my work is helping others and giving back. We only have so much time on this earth and that is my way of making the most of it.

Any other lessons you have learnt from grief to share?

Eleanor: Tons…too many to list. That's why we started "What's Your Grief."

Litsa: Grief never stops teaching you new lessons. All these years later I am still learning new lessons and new things about myself from the losses I have experienced.

Website:

www.whatsyourgrief.com

Chapter 21: Grief Lesson Stories - Mary Kate Cranston – Cry, Laugh, Heal

Grief Lesson Story

Introduction

My name is Mary Kate Cranston and I live in Washington, DC. At the age of 49, I became a widow and single parent. My husband had been sick for a number of years and after his death I thought I was prepared for what grief was going to feel like. I was totally wrong. It was much more devastating than I ever imagined. Somehow, through the help of a support group and the love of my family and friends, I went back to work, raised my son and found a new way of living.

As a former journalist, writing has always been a passion for me. I started writing my blog about grief and resilience as a way of giving back to those who helped me and also to extend a helping hand to others who are trying to heal after the loss of a loved one.

Ironically, grief has shown me that life can be a spontaneous adventure and we truly get the most out it when we fully embrace the possibilities of our journey.

What your site/project purpose is:

My blog is about sharing stories and helping others work through their grief by staying healthy, strengthening our emotional support systems and striving to become more resilient. Resilience, the ability to find hope in the midst of a personal crisis, fascinates and inspires me. The spirit of resilience inspired me to name my blog *Cry Laugh Heal* because of the circular and renewing effect of the three words: sometimes you can find yourself crying and you begin to laugh and other times you can be laughing and you begin to cry. Either way, both of these actions can help you heal and continue to rebuild your life.

Your Story of Grief

My husband died in his sleep at home in 2003. We had been married for 17 years and the last two and a half years were spent in and out of hospitals to treat his heart condition and diabetes. Our son was 13 years old when his father died and our reactions to his death were completely different. I couldn't stop crying and he couldn't stand to see me cry. I wanted to talk about his father constantly and he did not want to talk about him at all. It was a very painful time for both of us. I think we both felt very lost. He would go to school while I continued to work full-time to support us and somehow, slowly, we put one foot in front of the other and found our way to a place where we could find some peace with our loss.

What is the main lesson grief taught you about living?

Life is precious and can change faster than you realize. In the depth of my grief I wanted to go backwards in time to a place when my husband was alive but I knew that I couldn't do that. Living my life, day by day, forced me to go forward. I found that surprisingly life does somehow carry on. Grief can take you to some unpredictable places and my loss forced me to look at my life in a completely different way and ask myself what I really considered to be important. I stuck with those values even when others didn't understand what I was doing and it has given me comfort.

How did you come to find acceptance of the loss?

I don't think it was one event that proved to be the tipping point in helping me accept the death of my husband. I think it was a million little things that happened over a long period of time and the effect of those things ended up delivering me to a place where I knew I had to accept it. I couldn't change it and I couldn't fight it. I still miss my husband and I still have sad or painful feelings but I know, really know in my heart that he is gone even though there are times when I feel his presence. I have great faith in God and I believe that he loves us and will take care of us.

What advice would you give to someone who has experienced loss recently?

As painful as it is to do, you have to face your grief and allow yourself to mourn. I know you want to ignore it, push it down and forget about it by numbing yourself but unfortunately that only makes it worse. I think the hardest part of grieving is realizing that no one can do it for you. You must reach out to others who care about you for support and you have to dig deep within yourself to find the resources to heal yourself.

Be kind to yourself by making sure that you eat well, try to sleep whenever you can and take walks. I found walking, either with a friend or by myself to be therapeutic. There was something about the fresh air and moving around outside and being with nature that gave me strength and helped me feel less isolated.

Listen to your inner voice and do what you feel comfortable doing. Listen to others but in the end, you know what works well for you.

Did anyone say anything to you or do anything for you during your time of grief that really helped you?

The biggest act of kindness for me was when people would listen.

I'm talking about the kind of listening where the other person is not distracted and doesn't constantly ask questions. I joined a support group and met others who were also trying to rebuild their lives and this gave me relief and hope. I remember listening to one of our group leaders who had been widowed for more than a decade. She talked about her life as it is now and I would wonder how she was able to go on and seem so normal in her outlook about life. I found myself saying that if she could do it, then so could I!

Finding people I could trust and who would listen to me made all the difference.

What is your philosophy of grief?

There is no predictable schedule for grief. We all grieve differently because our relationship with the person who has died is different. You have to find what works for you. Maybe it's talking, maybe it's writing, maybe it's volunteering, or maybe it's meditating. Give yourself time, open yourself up to new opportunities and eventually hope will arise from your raw pain.

How has the pain transformed your life in a positive way with how you are now?

I try to be open to learning and doing new things. Sometimes you have to take a chance and try something you've never done before. What's the worst thing that can happen if it doesn't work out? I have made a fool out of myself many times but I also know it's not the end of the world if that happens. When someone that you love dearly has died you realize that you can't wait for things to happen to you. Sometimes you have to be the agent of change.

Any other lessons you have learnt from grief to share and assist others?

The human heart is an amazing organ. We fall in love, break up, and then perhaps fall in love over and over again, testing the resilience of our courageous hearts. Somehow, throughout our lives, we ride this emotional rollercoaster and our hearts manage to survive and keep on beating. When a relationship doesn't work out, we are sad but eventually we pick ourselves up and carry on until we meet the next person who catches our fancy.

But when your loved one dies, it truly feels as though you heart has broken into a million pieces and the first thing you want to do is shut it down forever…because you never want to feel that kind of pain ever again. You don't want to be vulnerable to feelings so intense you feel like you might die yourself, and there was a time when I did feel that way.

Then slowly, I began to heal and realize that life is about trusting your feelings and taking chances, losing and finding happiness and appreciating the incredible memories that were made with your loved one.

In the face of loss, it is even more important that we keep our hearts open to love. For love is what brings excitement to our lives!

Website:

www.crylaughheal.com

Twitter:

twitter.com/crylaughheal

Chapter 22: Grief Lesson Stories - Rose Duffy – Carry On

Grief Lesson Story

I am a songwriter, sax player and singer who wants nothing more than to make a difference in this world with my music. My latest song is called *Carry On*. *Carry On* is a tribute to our loved ones who are in Heaven. The lyrics are healing and uplifting. Singing along to this song helps you to connect more with your special angel who is up in Heaven. There is a very inspirational back-story as to how *Carry On* came about. You can find the video to this story on my music website.

Carry On has different meanings: To carry on the best that you know how, to carry on the memories of your loved one, and to carry on your loved one's legacy. I have received beautiful notes from people from all over the world, thanking me for this song's message. It has been the most rewarding musical experience I've ever had, and I am hoping that this song helps you as well.

Your experience of grief:

My Dad passed away when I was only 29 years old. He was always very supportive of me and my music. I was his "little rosebud." I lost my Dad way too soon. He was a kind man, with a tremendous and loving heart. As hard as it was, I was glad that I was there with my Mom and my siblings when our Dad passed away. It strengthened my faith in God. Our Dad had been in a coma for a few weeks. He could not hold his head up, and he could not speak at all. Just before our Dad was called up to Heaven, he became very aware of his surroundings and he opened his eyes wide open. We all shouted out "We love you, Dad!" It took several seconds for our Dad to say this, but he managed to get out the words "I .... love............. .... you .... too." After he said this, he magically lifted his head up, and he looked straight up to Heaven. It was very powerful. There was and still is no doubt in my mind that our Dad has been experiencing pure bliss up in Heaven ever since he took his last breath here on earth.

My Mom passed away ten years ago. She was a lot of fun and a nurturing Mom. We had a similar experience with our Mom. She was not able to speak for a couple weeks before she passed away. Soon before she passed away, she called out my name. I stepped up to be by our Mom and took her hand. She squeezed my hand and said "Thank you." She didn't always show appreciation for some of the things I did for her. It was important for her to thank me before she left for Heaven, and it meant the world to me.

What is the main lesson grief taught you about living?
I have six siblings. What I learned through the death of both my parents is that everybody grieves differently and in different stages. Nobody should ever tell somebody that they should just "get over it" or that they should "move on with their life." Each individual should be allowed to grieve in his/her own way and at his/her own pace.

How did you come to find acceptance of the loss?
Witnessing the death of my Mom and Dad made me see that they were no longer in pain. They are in paradise. They're eternally in paradise. I want to live my life to the fullest and in a loving way so that someday I will be able to join them in paradise.

What advice would you give to someone who has experienced loss recently?
My best advice is for them to ask God on a daily basis to give them the strength they need to endure their pain. The best thing to do is to seek God before you step out of bed in the morning.

Did anyone say anything to you or do anything for you during your time of grief that really helped you?

My friend gave me a card years ago that I have kept close to me in my nightstand. It says, "Today, Lord, let my life be a prayer. Let me be so close to you that you become a part of my every conversation. Let me be open to your presence so that I sense your power at work in the world you created. Let me be so filled with your love that it flows out to others. Today, Lord today, let my life be a prayer."

What is your philosophy of grief?

After going through all the stages of grief, I finally did get to the point where I realized that neither of my parents wanted me to continue to be sad about their passing. I remember driving in my car when my eyes were drawn to the license plate on the car ahead of me. It read, "Misery is an option." That was the turning point for me.

How has the pain transformed your life in a positive way with how you are now?

I went through a painful divorce (which is a big form of grief). I always maintained that I was going to turn a negative into a positive. I wrote an empowering, motivational song called *All About to Change*. This song has helped many people strive to become the person they want to be (after escaping from a bad relationship). I have also included a music video to *All About to Change* on my music website.

Any other lessons you have learnt from grief to share and assist others?

Since I lost my parents at such a young age, I have made it a point to spend as much time with my kids as possible and to create lasting memories with them. I wrote a song for my son when he graduated from college. It has a positive message for parents to spend lots of time with their kids. They grow up fast. This song is called *Big Picture Window*. It is also on my music website.

To all of you, I pray for your strength, peace and that you're surrounded with love. Let's all *Carry On*.

Website:
www.RoseDuffyMusic.com

Twitter:
twitter.com/RoseDuffyMusic

Facebook:
www.facebook.com/RoseDuffyMusic

Conclusion

Many people shared stories about my Mum after her death, and there was one common theme. She was a lady of compassion, love, light, and a great listener.

With this knowledge, I can fully embrace the memories of my Mum as she lives on in my life and as I fulfill my purpose. As I look back at the times of my greatest suffering, I realized those times were also life's greatest gifts.

I now feel a connection to my Mum that's close and strong because I live a life full of compassion, travel, love, and transformation. Her gift to me was my purpose in life. Pain is opportunity. Grief can become gratitude. Embrace love and life again to truly honour who you are.

I have discovered some key principles that changed my life and if you would like to discover them by working with me one to one and transform your pain back into love, feel free to find out more here: http://www.tomletgo.com.

It is possible for you to see grief from a new perspective, to be able to use the pain that grief causes as an opportunity to love and feel gratitude again in your life. From this point you can unlock your purpose and passion because you my friend, are a special and unique individual. There will only ever be one of you.

You will be able to:
- *Use your pain in a positive way*
- *Speak about the one you lost with gratitude and love*

– *Use your pain to assist others.*
– *Transform your grief from affecting your everyday life*
– *Understand, deal more clearly, and even find the positives of loss*
– *Discover who you are and what you are here to do.*
– *Live the rest of your life knowing your why you feel the pain you do as well as being able to honour your love one*
– *Find the love and connection in your life again.*
– *Turn your grief into greatness*

Life is all about growing and becoming stronger, not letting our pain break us down. You have a choice to empower yourself from grief into greatness.

In this book I share my personal journey with you from the diagnoses of my Mum's cancer until her passing, next through the grief and pain, then finally to the greatness I have found within. I share with you throughout the book key things that changed my life from pain and hurt to love and gratitude.

It hasn't been an easy journey and sometimes very lonely but I want you to know you can feel connection and love again. You have a greatness within and a unique gift to share with the world. My process will assist you to go from grief to greatness in your life.

Bonus: Subscribe To The Free Monthly Grief Hangout On Google+

When you subscribe to the grief hangout via email, you will get free access to a toolbox of exclusive subscriber-only resources plus access to our live online monthly grief hangout. All you have to do is enter your email address to the right to get instant access.

This resource will help you to hear about other experiences of grief and be able to give you tools to assist you on your journey. I'm always adding new resources to the toolbox as well, which you will be notified of as a subscriber. These will help you live life to the fullest and go from grief to greatness in your life.

Get instant access to these incredible tools and resources here: *http://www.tomletgo.com/griefhangout*

Final Thought

Thank you again for downloading this book!

I hope this book was able to help you identify with your experience from reading about others who have used their grief and experiences to transform their lives.

I hope it has left you with some realizations in your own experience and given you some hope with your own journey.

The next step is to apply some of the wisdom shared in the book and as a free gift I would like to share my other book *Words Through Grief* which you can download for free from here.

http://www.tomletgo.com/wordsthroughgrief

Finally, if you enjoyed this book, please take the time to share your thoughts and post a comment.

9454834R00068

Printed in Great Britain
by Amazon.co.uk, Ltd.,
Marston Gate.